SOUTH SHORE
TASTES

Recipes from the Best Restaurants
on Nova Scotia's South Shore

with Liz Feltham

Photographs by

Scott Munn

NIMBUS
PUBLISHING

For Mike, who makes me laugh every day.
—Liz Feltham

Nimbus Publishing Limited
PO Box 9166, Halifax, NS B3K 5M8
(902) 455-4286 www.nimbus.ca

Printed and bound in China

Liz Feltham photo: Mike Feltham
Scott Munn photo: Amy Belanger

Library and Archives Canada Cataloguing in Publication

Feltham, Liz
South shore tastes : recipes from the best
restaurants on Nova Scotia's south shore /
Liz Feltham ; illustrator: Scott Munn.

ISBN 978-1-55109-751-0

1. Cookery—Nova Scotia South Shore (Region).
2. Restaurants—Nova Scotia—South Shore (Region).
I. Munn, Scott II. Title.

TX715.6.F45 2010   641.59716'2   C2009-907281-5

We acknowledge the financial support of the Government of Canada through
the Book Publishing Industry Development Program (BPIDP) and the Canada
Council, and of the Province of Nova Scotia through the Department of
Tourism, Culture and Heritage for our publishing activities.

table of contents

introduction

The history of Nova Scotia's South Shore is inextricably entwined with the sea. Fishing towns and villages sprinkle the coast from Peggy's Cove to Yarmouth—communities built around wharves and lighthouses and tucked into the myriad of bays and coves that provide shelter from the North Atlantic.

It should come as no surprise, then, that the ocean and its bounty have greatly influenced the local cuisine in the region. Anything fished in the North Atlantic can be found on these shores, including shellfish like mussels, scallops, and lobster, and finfish like cod, haddock, pollock, and hake—the list is almost as endless as the seas themselves once seemed to be. Everyone on the South Shore has a favourite fishcake, chowder, or fisherman's pie recipe to make best use of the daily catch.

The South Shore's rich cultural heritage has also played a role in shaping the local culinary palette. The area's first European inhabitants were the French, although their settlements were sparse since the land was not as agriculturally rich as the fertile valleys farther inland. Next came the English, whose early immigration initiatives resulted in an influx of Swiss and German colonists. The French influence is still found along the western end of the Lighthouse Route, as it turns by Yarmouth and runs into the French Shore's Evangeline Trail. Homestyle restaurants on this end will most surely have rappie pie and a hearty fricot on the menu. Midway to Lunenburg on the Lighthouse Route you're likely to spot a Swiss influence on the menu—perhaps in the form of a schnitzel or potato röschti. But it is the German influence that is most heavily felt in the place names, accents, and, of course, cuisine of the South Shore—take, for example, the famous Tancook sauerkraut, a product of Mahone Bay's Tancook Island, where cabbages have been grown for just this purpose for over two hundred years, or the prevalence of braised meats such as sauerbraten or homemade sausages on local menus.

In recent years, the natural beauty of the South Shore has paved the way for a rise in tourism in the region. A wealth of bed and breakfasts, inns, and resorts has been established to cater to the flood of visitors coming to the area to view the incredible scenery, take part in popular ocean pastimes like sailing and whale watching, and enjoy simple pleasures like beachcombing and geocaching. Unsurprisingly, the blossoming tourism industry has brought with it a culinary evolution. While the South Shore is still home to traditional mom-and-pop restaurants that serve some of the best pan-fried haddock, chowders, and lobster rolls to be had anywhere, now these diners stand side by side with fine-dining establishments that rival those in larger Canadian urban centres. These new restaurants boast some of the most skilled chefs in the province, many of whom focus on progressive cuisine made from the finest local ingredients. Local seafood will always take centre stage here, but artisan bakeries and wineries are beginning to garner widespread attention as well.

A drive along the breathtaking coastline of the South Shore takes the tourist or day-tripper past many of the eateries featured in this book. Why not take a culinary tour of the

region as you wind your way down the scenic Lighthouse Route? There's nothing better than experiencing a dish prepared fresh with locally sourced produce by the person who created it. If you're not able to visit the region in person, many of the talented culinarians who own these restaurants have fortunately agreed to share their favourite recipes with me for this book. I urge you to try them out—let the dishes you prepare evoke memories of a past visit or inspire you to dream of a future trip to this region of culinary riches.

Bon appétit!

soups and starters

Driving along the Lighthouse Route, stopping every once in a while to get out of the car to admire the spectacular ocean vistas and breathe in the salty sea air, is an easy way to work up an appetite. This shoreline-hugging road, which winds its way from Peggy's Cove to Yarmouth, makes a rolling dinner party easy—stop at one spot for a little nibble, enjoy a main course a little farther down the road, and treat yourself to dessert at your destination. This selection of starters offers up plenty of tasty options to whet your appetite.

mako shark bites

Locally caught, sustainable mako shark served in this playful way can encourage even the most timid taste buds to enjoy a shark bite.

Makes 4 servings.

2 cups canola oil
1/2 cup milk
1 cup panko (Japanese bread crumbs)
1 pound fresh mako shark steaks*, cut into
  2-inch cubes and chilled
Salt to taste
Pepper to taste

Pour the canola oil into a large pot or deep fryer and heat it to 400°F.

Set up the breading station. Pour the milk into one small bowl and the panko into a second small bowl.

Season the shark with salt and pepper. Dip each of the shark pieces first into the milk, then into the panko to coat it evenly with breading.

Drop the breaded shark pieces into the preheated oil and cook them until golden brown, about 5 to 7 minutes.

When cooked, remove the bites from the oil and place them on a plate lined with paper towels to drain. Pat the bites with another paper towel to remove the excess oil.

Serve the bites immediately with your favourite dipping sauce. The shark bites are very adaptable, and take many mayonnaise-based sauces well, but you can also try ranch dressing, salsa, or even plum sauce with them.

*Note: When buying mako shark, freshness is key. If there is even a slight ammonia-like smell to the shark, pass on it.

The Kilted Grillhouse
Bayport

homemade fishcakes

This East Coast classic is a great example of the home-cooked comfort food you'll find at Large Marge's.

Makes 8 cakes.

1 pound salt cod
2 pounds (about 6 to 8 medium-sized) potatoes, peeled and cubed
1 cup finely diced white onion
1/2 teaspoon dried summer savory
4 tablespoons butter
2 lemons, cut into wedges, for garnish (optional)
Prepared tartar sauce for garnish (optional)

Soak the fish in cold water overnight, changing the water several times throughout the soaking process.

Remove the salt cod from the soaking water and place it in a large pot over high heat. Fill the pot with enough water to cover the fish. Boil until the salt cod is flaky, about 20 minutes. Drain well and set aside.

Place the potatoes in a large pot and cover them with cold water. Place the pot over medium-high heat and bring the water to a boil. Cook until the potatoes can easily be pierced with a fork, about 20 minutes. Drain the potatoes and return them to the pot. Mash the potatoes with a potato masher or fork, and set aside to cool for 15 minutes.

Once the potatoes have cooled, combine the cod, mashed potatoes, onion, and summer savory in a large bowl. Divide the mixture evenly into patties and place the patties on a large plate. Cover the plate with plastic wrap and place it in the fridge. Let the patties rest in the fridge for a few minutes or overnight. (Fishcakes hold their shape better when allowed to rest).

thai squash soup

Proprietor Lynda Flinn says this easy soup is a favourite at the Kiwi Café. The amount of fragrant red curry paste used in the dish can be adjusted to accommodate any palate.

Makes 6 to 8 servings.

2 tablespoons extra virgin olive oil
2 large yellow onions, diced
1 tablespoon Thai red curry paste
8 cups vegetable stock✳
4 1/2 pounds butternut or other hard winter squash (about 1 large butternut squash or 2 medium buttercup squash), peeled and diced
Salt to taste
Pepper to taste
Sour cream for garnish (optional)
Fresh Thai basil for garnish (optional)

Warm the olive oil over medium heat in a large heavy-bottomed stock pot. Add the diced onions and cook, stirring occasionally, about 5 to 6 minutes or until softened but not browned. Add the Thai red curry paste and stir until blended. Continue cooking for 2 to 3 minutes. The onions should take on the reddish colour of the curry paste.

Pour the vegetable stock into the stock pot and bring the mixture to a boil. Add the diced squash and reduce the heat to medium-low. Simmer uncovered until the squash is tender, about 20 to 30 minutes.

Place the mixture in a food processor or blender and purée until smooth, about 2 to 5 minutes. Stir in salt and pepper to taste.

Return the soup to the pot and warm over medium heat before serving.

To serve, ladle the soup into bowls and garnish each serving with a dollop of sour cream and a sprig of Thai basil.

✳Note: If using store-bought vegetable stock, try to use a low-sodium variety.

Kiwi Café
Chester

smoked haddock and seafood chowder

Just add a crusty roll or a thick slab of multigrain bread to take this chowder from appetizer to main course.

Makes 8 servings.

1 tablespoon vegetable oil
1/2 pound smoked haddock, minced
1 1/2 cups onions, diced
1 1/2 carrots, diced
1 1/2 medium-sized Yukon Gold potatoes, diced
1/2 pound raw scallops (60/110 count*)
1/2 pound raw shrimp (150/250 count*), peeled and deveined
2 pounds raw mussels, removed from shells
1 cup flour
4 cups 35% whipping cream (heavy cream)
4 cups milk
Fresh chives, chopped, for garnish (optional)

Warm the oil in a large, heavy-bottomed soup pot over medium heat. Add the haddock, onions, carrots, and potatoes and sauté, stirring often, about 30 to 45 minutes, or until the vegetables are just tender.

While the vegetables are cooking, prepare the scallops, shrimp, and mussels. In a medium-sized saucepan, bring 4 to 6 cups of water to a boil. Add the shrimp and cook

3 minutes, just until the shrimp are pink. Remove the shrimp and set aside. Bring the water back to a boil. Add the scallops and cook for 2 minutes. Drain the scallops, reserving 1 cup of the water. Set the scallops aside with the shrimp. Bring the cup of water back to a boil and add the mussels. Cover the saucepan and steam the mussels 5 to 8 minutes, or until they have opened. Drain the mussels and set aside with the scallops and shrimp.

Once the haddock and vegetable mixture has finished cooking, remove the pot from heat and stir in the flour. Add the cream and milk and stir to combine. Place the pot back on the burner and increase the heat to high. Bring the mixture to a boil.

Add the cooked scallops, shrimp, and mussels to the boiling haddock mixture. Reduce the heat to medium-low and cook, stirring often, until the shellfish are warmed through, about 8 to 10 minutes.

To serve, ladle the chowder into large soup cups and garnish each cup with chopped fresh chives.

*Note: Because the sizes of scallops and shrimp vary widely from place to place, they are most often sold by "count" instead of by size. A "count" indicates the number of shrimp or scallops per pound. For example, a 10/20 count of scallops means that there are 10 to 20 in a pound, while a U10 count indicates that there are less than 10 in a pound. The lower the count is, the bigger the shrimp or scallops are.

Salt Shaker Deli
Lunenburg

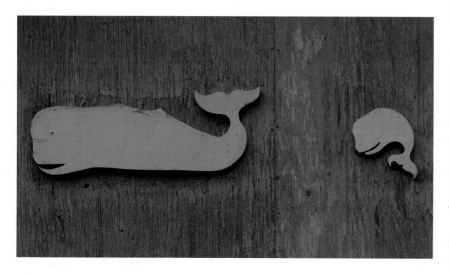

ruisseau oysters in fresh tomato marinade

The intensely flavoured, plump, juicy Ruisseau oysters hold up very well against the acidic tomato marinade in this dish.

Makes 6 servings.

3 ripe medium tomatoes, quartered, or 4
   ripe plum tomatoes, halved
1/2 lemon, juice and zest
1/2 teaspoon sea salt, or sea salt to taste
1/8 teaspoon freshly ground black pepper
2 teaspoons Worcestershire sauce
1 teaspoon Tabasco or other Louisiana-style
   hot sauce
1 tablespoon chopped fresh lovage or
   parsley
6 Ruisseau or other large local oysters,
   shucked
6 golden oregano leaves for garnish
   (optional)

Using a food mill*, juice the tomatoes into a small non-metallic bowl. Add the lemon juice and zest, sea salt, pepper, Worcestershire sauce, hot sauce, and lovage or parsley and mix well.

To serve, place each of the shucked oysters in a chilled martini glass or other fancy glass. Gently ladle one-sixth of the marinade mixture over each oyster. Chill for at least 10 minutes. When ready to serve, top each glass with a golden oregano leaf or other garnish of your choice. Oyster lovers may want to "shoot" the oyster and liquid directly from the glass, but the oysters can certainly be spooned out as well.

*Note: Food mills are now readily available at most department stores and kitchen supply stores. If you don't have one, process the tomatoes in a blender or food processor until liquefied, about 2 to 4 minutes. Strain the tomatoes through a sieve to remove the seeds before using.

Trout Point Lodge of Nova Scotia
East Kemptville

mediterranean shrimp

Flavours from both sides of the Atlantic combine in this dish, one of The Rope Loft's most popular appetizers.

Makes 4 servings.

4 teaspoons garlic butter
24 raw shrimp (16/20 count), shelled and deveined
1 cup white wine
2 large tomatoes, diced
3 teaspoons dried oregano
1 cup feta cheese

Preheat the oven to 400°F.

Melt the garlic butter in an ovenproof skillet over high heat. Add the shrimp and sear just until no longer pink, about 2 to 3 minutes. Add the wine and sauté for 1 or 2 more minutes. Using tongs, turn the shrimp to coat them evenly with the wine-butter sauce.

Remove the skillet from the heat. Top the shrimp mixture with the tomatoes, oregano, and feta cheese and place the skillet in the oven. Bake until the mixture has warmed through and the cheese has begun to melt, about 5 minutes.

Serve the dish directly in the skillet* with focaccia or other Mediterranean flatbread on the side.

*Note: Take caution, as the skillet will likely still be hot from the oven. If possible, wrap the skillet handle in a towel or other covering when serving and eating the dish to avoid burns.

The Rope Loft
Chester

mains from the sea

Working fishing villages all along the Lighthouse Route feature restaurants with seaside views that give diners the exceptional experience of watching over boats bobbing gently alongside docks and knowing these very same boats brought their dinners ashore that day. In the following recipes, local seafood is showcased in numerous ways to show off its versatility.

shrimp and smoked salmon pasta

The robust flavour of the Nova Scotia smoked salmon holds up well against the rich sauce in this dish.

Makes 2 servings.

3 tablespoons butter
4 small button mushrooms, sliced
8 raw shrimp (31/35 count), peeled and
  deveined
1/8 cup sherry
1/2 cup 35% whipping cream (heavy cream)
1/4 cup shredded Asiago cheese
4 ounces smoked salmon, chopped
2 servings cooked linguini or fettuccine
Fresh parsley, chopped, for garnish
  (optional)

Melt the butter in a large skillet over medium heat. Add the mushrooms and sauté for 2 to 3 minutes, stirring often. Add the shrimp and sauté for another 2 to 3 minutes, or until the shrimp have turned pink. Stir in the sherry, cream, and Asiago cheese. Let the mixture simmer for 3 minutes.

Add the smoked salmon to the skillet and stir. Remove the skillet from heat and toss in the cooked pasta, continuing to toss until the pasta has warmed through.

To serve, place half of the pasta onto each of two pasta plates and garnish with chopped parsley.

Magnolia's Grill
Lunenburg

lobster rolls

In this recipe, Fredie's Fantastic Fish House franchise owner Tammy Fredericks reveals her secrets to a deceptively simple lobster roll: a fresh roll and coleslaw dressing instead of mayonnaise.

Makes 2 rolls.

Coleslaw Dressing

1/2 cup mayonnaise
2 tablespoons cider vinegar
1 teaspoon white sugar
2 tablespoons milk
1 tablespoon celery seed

Place all ingredients in a large bowl and mix well. Refrigerate at least 12 hours before using.

Lobster Rolls

1 pound (about 2/3 cup) cooked lobster meat
Coleslaw Dressing to taste (see recipe opposite)
2 fresh rectangular-shaped rolls
2/3 cup shredded Boston lettuce

Combine the lobster meat with dressing to taste in a small bowl. The dressing should coat the meat, but not be too runny.

Split the roll in half lengthwise, leaving one side attached. Line the inside of the roll with the lettuce. Spoon the dressed lobster into the roll on top of the lettuce and close the roll.

Serve as is or with fresh hand-cut fries—and don't forget a napkin!

Fredie's Fantastic Fish House
Upper Tantallon

shrimp and scallop stuffed lobster tails

This rich dish is a fitting showcase for fresh Nova Scotia shellfish, not to mention a tourist favourite at The Quarterdeck.

Makes 2 servings.

6 raw shrimp*, peeled, deveined, and chopped coarsely
4 raw scallops*, chopped coarsley
3/4 cup mozzarella cheese, grated
4 tablespoons melted garlic butter, divided
2 (4-ounce) lobster tails, raw with shell on
1/2 cup bread crumbs

Preheat the oven to 400°F.

Combine the shrimp, scallops, mozzarella cheese, and 2 tablespoons of the garlic butter in a large mixing bowl. Cover and refrigerate for at least 15 minutes.

While the seafood mixture is chilling, split the lobster tails down the middle lengthwise, cutting through the top of the shell but not all the way through to the bottom. Clean the tails well by rinsing under cold running water.

Once the seafood mixture has finished chilling, divide it into two equal parts. Holding the split tails open slightly, spoon each portion of mixture into one of the splits. The stuffing should overflow.

Place the lobster tails on a cookie sheet and sprinkle the tops with the bread crumbs. Bake the tails for approximately 25 minutes, or just until the crumbs start to brown.

Serve the lobster tails with the remaining garlic butter.

*Note: Because the shrimp and scallops are being chopped for this recipe, you don't have to be too specific about the size— anything in the medium-sized range will work well.

The Quarterdeck Beachside Villas and Grill
Summerville Beach

planked maple salmon with port-balsamic glaze

*A signature dish at Oak Island Resort, this is best made over an open fire.
If that's not an option, a barbecue will do nicely.*

Makes 2 servings.

Salmon

1/4 pound butter
1/4 cup maple syrup
2 (6-ounce) Atlantic salmon fillets
2 cedar planks, soaked in water overnight*
Sea salt to taste
Freshly ground black pepper to taste
Port-Balsamic Glaze (see recipe, below)

Preheat the barbecue to 400°F or prepare an open campfire.

Melt the butter in a small, heavy-bottomed saucepan. Add the maple syrup and stir until well blended. Allow the maple butter to cool to room temperature.

Place each of the salmon fillets on a cedar plank and brush them liberally with the maple butter. Season the salmon to taste with the sea salt and freshly ground black pepper.

Set the cedar planks on the preheated barbecue and cover them with aluminum pie pans or tents of tinfoil.

Allow the salmon to bake under the foil cover, occasionally moving the plank around to cooler spots on the grill to allow the smoke flavour to penetrate more thoroughly. Bake the salmon until it is cooked to your preferred degree of doneness. (As there are so many variables when cooking over a grill, it is hard to give a specific amount of time, but the test kitchen produced a medium-rare fillet over white-hot coals in 10 minutes.)

When the salmon is cooked to your liking, use a wide spatula to slide it off the plank and onto your plate.

Port-Balsamic Glaze

2 cups port wine
2 cups balsamic vinegar
1 cup sugar

Combine the port wine, balsamic vinegar, and sugar in a large, heavy-bottomed saucepan over medium-low heat. Cook uncovered, stirring often, for about 20 minutes, or until the liquid has reduced to a syrupy texture (it should coat the back of a wooden spoon lightly when ready). Let the glaze cool before serving.

To serve the dish, place the salmon fillet on a serving plate and drizzle it with Port-Balsamic Glaze. Accompany it with basmati rice and fresh seasonal vegetables.

*Note: Ensure that your cedar planks are food-safe. Food-safe cedar planks are now readily available at most major supermarkets, cut in single sizes. When washed properly, they can be used several times.

Oak Island Resort
Western Shore

scallops with fava bean purée

The menu changes frequently at Chef Martin Ruiz Salvador's internationally acclaimed Fleur de Sel dining room, so you may not see this dish on offer should you visit—but not to worry, there's sure to be something equally pleasing.

Makes 4 servings.

2 pounds fresh fava beans
4 shallots, diced, divided
4 tablespoons plus 1/4 cup extra virgin olive oil, divided
1 tablespoon lemon juice
1 (1/2-pound) slab smoked bacon, diced
12 fingerling potatoes, halved lengthwise
24 large scallops (20/30 count)
Fleur de sel for garnish (optional)
Fresh chervil for garnish (optional)

In a large pot or steamer, steam the fava beans for about 1 minute to loosen the skins. Once the skins are loosened, remove the beans from heat and allow them to cool enough to be easily handled. Remove the beans from their pods by cutting a slit in the seam of each pod and sliding the beans out into a bowl. Discard the pods.

Place the fava beans, half of the diced shallots, the 4 tablespoons of olive oil, and the lemon juice in a food processor and blend until smooth, about 2 to 3 minutes. Set aside.

Place the smoked bacon, the remaining diced shallots, and the fingerling potatoes in a large sauté pan over medium heat. Sauté the mixture until the bacon is cooked and the potatoes are tender, about 8 to 12 minutes. Set aside and keep warm.

Heat the 1/4 cup of olive oil in a large non-stick pan. Place the scallops in the pan and sear both sides until golden brown, about 30 seconds per side.

To serve, reheat the fava bean purée in the microwave for 30 seconds on high heat. Spoon one-quarter of the warmed fava bean purée onto each of four plates. Lay 6 potato halves on top of each serving of fava beans, flesh side up. Spread a quarter of the remaining bacon and shallots around the potatoes on each dish. Place 6 scallops—each one atop a potato—on each plate. Garnish the dishes with fleur de sel and sprigs of chervil.

Fleur de Sel Restaurant et Maison Lunenburg

scallops with orange sesame ginger drizzle

Roland Glauser, Charlotte Lane Café's owner/chef, introduces the Near East to the Far East in this Asian-inspired dish.

Makes 4 servings.

1 cup orange marmalade
1/3 cup fresh lime juice
1/8 cup Asian fish sauce
1/3 cup mirin rice wine
1/8 cup fresh chopped ginger
1/2 tablespoon Chinese hot sauce
1/8 cup sesame oil
1/8 cup Worcestershire sauce
1 small carrot, peeled and finely grated
1 teaspoon cornstarch
1 teaspoon water
2 tablespoons canola oil
1 pound fresh scallops (10/20 count)

Combine the marmalade, lime juice, fish sauce, mirin, ginger, hot sauce, sesame oil, Worcestershire sauce, and carrot in a small saucepan over medium heat. Bring the mixture to a boil.

Meanwhile, in a separate bowl, mix the cornstarch with the water until you have a thin paste (add more water if necessary). Slowly pour the cornstarch paste into the boiling sauce mixture, stirring constantly, until the sauce begins to thicken. Remove the sauce from heat and set aside.

Heat the canola oil in a large skillet over high heat. Place the scallops in the oil and sear, turning once, until golden brown on each side, about 30 seconds per side.

To serve, divide the scallops among four plates and drizzle each plate with Orange Sesame Ginger sauce.

Charlotte Lane Café
Shelburne

mains from the land

Should you grow tired of the surfeit of surf in your travels, you can take a break with some turf. Local lamb, pork, and free-range chicken are all common in Lighthouse Route kitchens. Although the South Shore is not as rich in agricultural land as some neighbouring counties, local farmers have managed to supply area residents and restaurants alike. Local lamb, when in season, is not to be missed. In this section, you'll find a simple, classic recipe that showcases its flavour. You'll also find recipes for hearty pork and summery barbecue ribs that are fantastic year-round.

nova scotia lamb with cranberry-blueberry compote

The distinct, sweet flavour of Nova Scotia grass-fed lamb pairs beautifully with the tart berry compote in this dish.

Makes 2 servings.

1 1/2 cups frozen cranberries
1/2 cup water
3/4 cup sugar
1 cup frozen blueberries
6 (2- to 3-ounce) Nova Scotia lamb chops
4 tablespoons extra virgin olive oil
Salt to taste
Pepper to taste

Combine the cranberries, water, and sugar in a small, heavy-bottomed saucepan. Simmer over medium heat for 45 minutes to 1 hour, or until the mixture begins to cook and thicken. Add the blueberries, stirring until heated through. Remove the compote from heat and set aside.

Preheat the barbecue to medium.

Rub the lamb chops with the olive oil, and season them liberally with salt and pepper. Grill the lamb chops, turning occasionally, just to an internal temperature of 140°F. This will give you a medium-rare chop. (More than this could toughen your lamb.)

To serve, place each lamb chop on a plate and top it with warm Cranberry-Blueberry Compote (you may need to re-warm the compote before serving). Accompany each serving with roasted rosemary new potatoes and local seasonal vegetables (try asparagus in the spring and parsnip in the winter).

Lane's Privateer Inn
Liverpool

pork steak with pommery mustard sauce

The robust Pommery Mustard Sauce is really the star of this dish. It also goes equally well with roasted chicken.

Makes 2 servings.

4 teaspoons canola oil
1 (1 1/2-pound) pork top loin steak, trimmed of fat
Salt to taste
Pepper to taste
4 teaspoons unsalted butter
3 large shallots, finely chopped
8 button mushrooms, quartered
1/4 cup red wine
2 tablespoons pommery or grainy mustard
3 tablespoons 35% whipping cream (heavy cream)
1 sprig rosemary, finely chopped
2 tablespoons parsley, finely chopped

Preheat the oven to 350°F.

Warm the canola oil in a large frying pan over medium-high heat. Season the pork steak with salt and pepper to taste. Place the pork in the heated oil, and sear until brown on both sides. Remove the pork from the heat and place it in a roasting pan. Roast uncovered until an internal temperature of 160°F is reached. When the roast is finished, remove the pan from the oven and allow the pork to stand for 5 minutes (this allows the juices to be reabsorbed).

While the pork is roasting, prepare the Pommery Mustard Sauce. Melt the butter in a medium-sized pan over medium heat. Add the shallots and mushrooms and sauté until soft, about 3 to 5 minutes. Stir in the red wine, mustard, cream, and rosemary. Cook, stirring constantly, until the sauce thickens slightly, about 8 to 10 minutes. Add the parsley and salt and pepper to taste and stir to combine.

To serve the dish, cut the pork steak in half and place one portion of pork on each plate. Spoon half of the Pommery Mustard Sauce over each serving. Accompany the pork with a scoop of creamy garlic mashed potatoes.

Chez Bruno's Café and Bistro
Yarmouth

baby back ribs with hickory smoke barbecue sauce

Finger-lickin' barbecue, salt spray splashing against the rocks at Peggy's Cove—now this is summer!

Makes 4 servings.

4 slabs pork back ribs
4 cups brown sugar
1 teaspoon salt
1 tablespoon onion powder
1 teaspoon white pepper
1 tablespoon garlic powder
1 1/2 cups water
4 cups ketchup
1 tablespoon prepared mustard
1/8 cup liquid hickory smoke

Place the ribs in large stock pot over high heat and cover them with water. Bring the water to a boil. Reduce the heat to medium and simmer, uncovered, until the ribs are tender, about 1 1/2 to 2 hours.

While the ribs are cooking, prepare the Hickory Smoke Barbecue Sauce. Place the remaining ingredients in a large non-metallic bowl and whisk them together well. Refrigerate the barbecue sauce until ready to use.

When the ribs have finished simmering, remove them from the water using a pair of large metal tongs. Place the ribs on the barbecue over a low flame and coat them liberally with the Hickory Smoke Barbecue Sauce. Grill until the sauce has penetrated the meat and caramelized, about 30 to 45 minutes.

To serve, place each slab of ribs on a large plate. Accompany each serving with a baked potato, coleslaw, and plenty of wet naps for sticky fingers.

The Sou'Wester Restaurant and Gift Shop
Peggy's Cove

classic italian osso bucco

Trattoria Della Nonna's chef/owner, Terry Vassallo, says this hearty dish is a favourite at the restaurant, even in midsummer heat—the richness of the veal marrow knows no seasonal boundaries.

Makes 4 servings.

1/4 cup extra virgin olive oil
4 (1 1/2-inch-thick) veal shanks*
4 cups diced onion
4 cups diced celery
3 cups diced carrot
6 cloves garlic, crushed
8 cups high-quality veal, chicken, or beef stock
2 cups red wine
2 large cans high-quality Italian tomatoes
2 tablespoons chopped fresh wild oregano
2 tablespoons chopped fresh wild thyme

Preheat the oven to 250°F.

Warm the olive oil in a large braising pot or Dutch oven over medium heat. Place the veal shanks in the oil one at a time and brown on each side, about 5 minutes per shank. Set the shanks aside.

Place the onion, celery, and carrot in the braising pot, and sauté slowly over medium heat, stirring often, until tender, about 45 minutes. Stir in the garlic and sauté 2 to 3 minutes more. Return the veal shanks to the pot and stir in the stock, wine, and tomatoes. Add the chopped oregano and thyme and bring to a boil.

Cover the pot and place it in the preheated oven. Bake until the meat is tender but not falling off the bone, about 5 1/2 hours.

To serve, place each of the veal shanks on a serving plate and accompany with Asiago risotto and wilted rapini (this bitter green helps cut through the richness of the rest of the dish).

*Note: For this recipe, the thickness of the shank is more important than the weight.

Trattoria Della Nonna Ristaurante e Pizzaria Lunenburg

maple curry chicken ravioli

The Nova Scotia maple syrup lends a gentle undertone of sweetness to the mild curry flavour in this dish.

Makes 2 servings.

3 tablespoons vegetable oil, divided
1 pound boneless, skinless chicken breasts
    (about two medium-sized breasts)*, cut
    into 1-inch cubes
2/3 cup finely chopped onion
2 cloves garlic, chopped
2 tablespoons minced fresh ginger
1/4 cup cream cheese
2 tablespoons mild curry paste
1 cup chicken stock
2 cups 35% whipping cream (heavy cream)
1 teaspoon Montreal steak spice
1/4 cup Nova Scotia maple syrup
16 pieces cooked ravioli (any vegetable-
    stuffed ravioli will do)

Warm 1 tablespoon of the vegetable oil in a large non-stick skillet over medium heat. Add the chicken and cook, stirring occasionally, until the chicken is no longer pink, about 20 minutes. Set aside.

Heat the remaining vegetable oil in a large saucepan over medium heat. Add the onion, garlic, and ginger and sauté until tender, about 5 minutes. Add the cream cheese and curry paste, stirring until smooth. Stir in the chicken stock, whipping cream, steak spice, and maple syrup. Simmer, uncovered, 3 to 5 minutes to reduce the liquid slightly.

Add the ravioli and cooked chicken pieces to the sauce, and simmer until heated through, about 6 to 8 minutes.

To serve, place 8 ravioli pieces in each of two large pasta bowls and spoon the desired amount of sauce overtop. Accompany with garlic toast or naan.

*The chicken in this dish can be any combination of cooked white or dark meat—this is an excellent way to use up leftover chicken!

White Point Beach Resort
White Point

strawberry chicken salad with citrus poppy seed dressing

Sweet berry and tart citrus notes can make the most jaded palate sing in this main-course salad.

Makes 4 salads.

Citrus Poppy Seed Dressing

1/2 cup mayonnaise
1/2 cup 35% whipping cream (heavy cream)
2 tablespoons liquid honey
1/8 cup concentrated orange juice, not diluted
1 tablespoon lemon juice
1 tablespoon roasted poppy seeds
Freshly ground pepper to taste

Combine the mayonnaise, cream, honey, orange juice, lemon juice, and poppy seeds in a large bowl. If desired, mix in freshly ground pepper to taste. Refrigerate until ready to use. (Dressing may be kept, tightly sealed and refrigerated, for 2 to 3 days.)

Strawberry Chicken Salad

1 pound boneless, skinless chicken breasts (about 2 medium-sized breasts)
Salt to taste
Pepper to taste
1 tablespoon canola oil
10 ounces mesclun greens
Citrus Poppyseed Dressing to taste (see recipe, opposite)
16 large local strawberries, sliced
4 tablespoons sliced toasted almonds

Preheat the barbecue to high.

Season the chicken breasts with salt and pepper to taste. Rub the seasoned breasts with the canola oil.

Place the chicken breasts on the barbecue and grill for 5 minutes. Turn the breasts and allow them to cook until an internal temperature of 180°F is reached. Remove the chicken breasts from the grill and cut them into 3/4-inch-wide slices. Set aside.

Place the mesclun greens in a large salad bowl. Gently toss the salad with Citrus Poppy Seed Dressing to taste (the greens should be thinly and evenly coated).

To serve, divide the salad onto four plates or bowls. Top each salad with one-quarter of the sliced strawberries, toasted almonds, and cooked chicken slices.

Lothar's Café
Shelburne

desserts

Of course you've saved room for dessert, or perhaps just a little sweet treat with your coffee or tea, at your final destination along the Lighthouse Route. This is the perfect time to sit back, relax, and enjoy the vistas the South Shore is famous for. From the timeless elegance of a baked Alaska to the down-home goodness of a berry grunt or buckle, any of these recipes can prove a most satisfying finale to a splendid South Shore feast.

Drop the dough mixture by spoonfuls onto the hot berry mixture. Cover the saucepan and simmer for 15 minutes over medium heat (do not open the lid while simmering or you may cause the grunt to fall!).

To serve, scoop the biscuits into bowls and top each serving with a large spoonful of the blueberry sauce. Accompany with ice cream or whipped cream.

Seaside Shanty Restaurant
& Chowder House
Chester Basin

south shore bumbleberry crisp

According to Wilma Raaymaker, proprietor of Trellis Café, bumbleberry is defined as follows: "Seven South Shore sumptuous surprises (blueberry, blackberry, raspberry, strawberry, rhubarb, apple, and cherry) in one Nova Scotia flavour!"

Makes 2 pies.

Pie Crusts

2 cups unbleached white flour
1 teaspoon salt
2/3 cup vegetable shortening
4 to 6 tablespoons cold water
1/2 beaten egg
1/4 teaspoon white vinegar

Sift the flour and salt together in a large mixing bowl. Using a pastry cutter or large fork, cut in the shortening and combine until the texture is crumbly.

In a separate small bowl, combine the water, egg, and vinegar and stir well.

Pour the wet ingredients into the dry mix, combining just until the dough comes together to form a ball. As with any pie crust, the less you mix, the more tender the finished product will be.

Divide the dough in half and roll each half out onto a lightly floured surface. Carefully pick up each dough circle and lay it over a 10-inch pie plate. Set aside until ready to use.

Bumbleberry Filling

5 cups frozen mixed berries (blueberries, raspberries, blackberries, and strawberries)
1 cup frozen blueberries
1 1/2 cups frozen chopped rhubarb
3 large apples, peeled and cubed
1/2 can cherry pie filling
2 cups sugar

Spread the frozen mixed berries out onto a cutting board and chop any large strawberries in half so that all pieces of fruit are about the same size. Transfer the mixed berries to a large bowl, and add the blueberries, rhubarb, apples, cherry pie filling, and sugar. Stir until uniformly mixed. Set aside until ready to use.

Crisp Topping

3 cups large-flake rolled oats
1/4 teaspoon salt
1/4 cup flour
1/4 teaspoon baking powder
1/8 teaspoon cinnamon
1/2 cup soft butter

Combine the rolled oats, salt, flour, baking powder, and cinnamon in a large mixing bowl. Add the butter and blend until the mixture is crumbly. Set aside until ready to use.

Preheat the oven to 350°F.

To assemble the crisp, pour half of the bumbleberry filling into each of the unbaked pie crusts. Top each pie with half of the crisp topping. Trim the excess dough from the sides of the pie pans.

Place the crisps in the preheated oven and bake for approximately 45 to 50 minutes, or until the crusts are golden brown and the fillings are bubbling. Remove the crisps from the oven and place them on a cooling rack until set, about 1 to 2 hours.

Serve slices of the crisp cold or warm with whipped cream. (Bumbleberry Crisp also makes a tasty morning treat when served with yogourt!)

Trellis Café
Hubbards

kafka cookies

In keeping with the literary surroundings of the café, many Biscuit Eater treats are named for authors. In this case, the dark and complex flavours of the cookies echo Kafka's personality.

Makes 12 cookies.

1 1/2 cups unbleached white flour
1/2 cup dark cocoa powder, plus extra for garnish
1 1/2 tablespoons finely ground espresso beans
1 cup butter
3/4 cup super-fine sugar
1 teaspoon pure vanilla extract

Preheat the oven to 350°F.

Sift the flour, 1/2 cup of cocoa powder, and ground espresso beans together in a large bowl.

Place the butter, sugar, and vanilla in a separate mixing bowl and beat with an electric mixer until creamy, about 3 to 4 minutes.

Gradually add the flour mixture into the butter mixture while beating with the electric mixer, scraping down sides of the bowl as you go. Beat the mixture for 3 to 5 minutes, or until it has come together to form a firm dough.

Grease two cookie sheets, or line them with parchment paper. Portion the dough evenly into 12 smooth, round balls and place the dough balls onto the cookie sheets about 2 inches apart.

Dip the tines of a fork into the extra cocoa powder, then use the tines to press down lightly on the dough balls to compress them slightly.

Place the cookies in the preheated oven and bake until just firm to the touch and the tops show a light cracking, about 13 to 16 minutes. Do not overbake.

Remove the cookies from the oven and let them rest on the cookie sheets for 2 to 3 minutes before transferring them to a cooling rack. Allow the cookies to cool for 10 to 15 minutes before serving.

The Biscuit Eater Café and Bookseller
Mahone Bay

cinnamon rolls

Elizabeth Brown, owner of the Woodpile Café, was generous enough to share this recipe for the café's signature sweet.

Makes 12 rolls.

2 cups all-purpose flour
4 teaspoons baking powder
1 teaspoon salt
1/2 cup butter, chilled, plus 1/4 cup butter, softened
1 cup milk
3/4 cup sugar
1/2 tablespoon cinnamon
Icing sugar for garnish (optional)

Preheat the oven to 400°F.

Sift the flour, baking powder, and salt together in a large mixing bowl. Using a pastry cutter or fork, cut the 1/2 cup of chilled butter into the flour mixture. Combine until the mixture is crumbly. Add the milk, stirring the mixture with a fork until it turns into a soft dough.

Turn the dough out onto a lightly floured surface and knead it gently for 8 to 10 minutes.

Roll the dough into a 9" x 20" rectangle. Brush the surface of the dough with the 1/4 cup of softened butter. Sprinkle the sugar and cinnamon evenly overtop.

Roll the dough up widthwise like a jelly roll to form a log. Slice the log widthwise into 12 small rolls.

Line a muffin tin with paper liners, and place each cinnamon roll into its own cup.

Place the muffin tin in the preheated oven and bake for approximately 15 minutes, or until the cinnamon roll tops are lightly browned. Remove the rolls from the oven. If desired, garnish the rolls with icing sugar.

Woodpile Carvings and Café
Liverpool

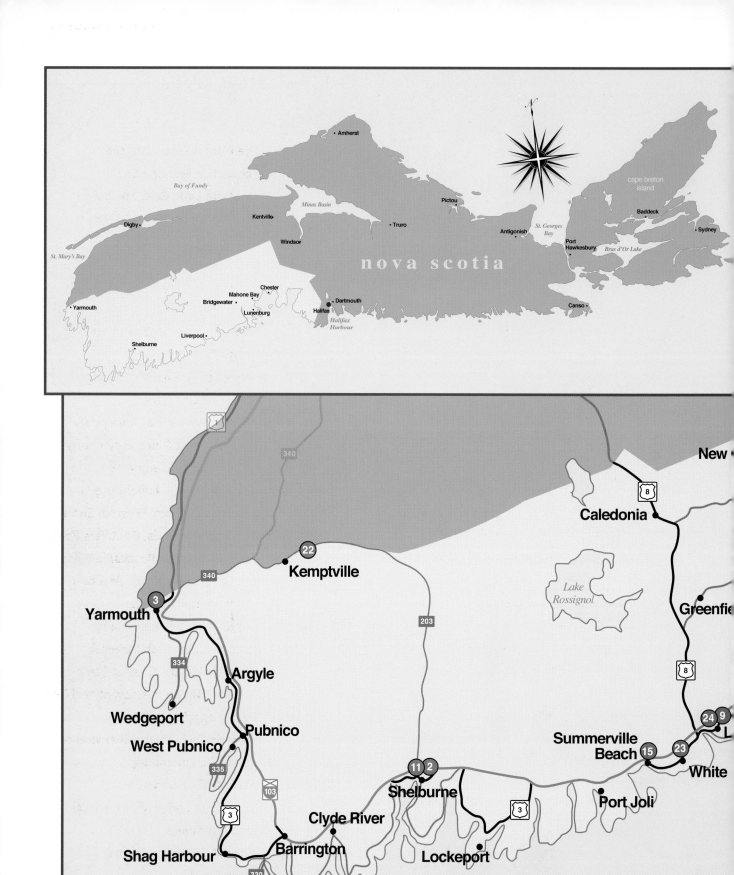

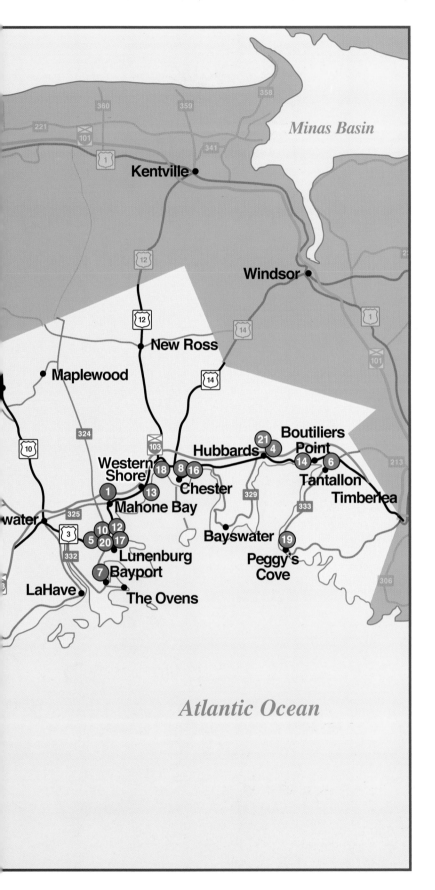

1. **The Biscuit Eater Café and Bookseller**, Mahone Bay
2. **Charlotte Lane Café**, Shelburne
3. **Chez Bruno's Café and Bistro**, Yarmouth
4. **Dauphinee Inn**, Hubbards
5. **Fleur de Sel Restaurant et Maison**, Lunenburg
6. **Fredie's Fantastic Fish House**, Upper Tantallon
7. **The Kilted Grillhouse**, Bayport
8. **Kiwi Café**, Chester
9. **Lane's Privateer Inn**, Liverpool
10. **Large Marge's Diner**, Lunenburg
11. **Lothar's Café**, Shelburne
12. **Magnolia's Grill**, Lunenburg
13. **Oak Island Resort**, Western Shore
14. **Oliver Southwoods**, Boutiliers Point
15. **The Quarterdeck Beachside Villas and Grill**, Summerville Beach
16. **The Rope Loft**, Chester
17. **Salt Shaker Deli**, Lunenburg
18. **Seaside Shanty Restaurant & Chowder House**, Chester Basin
19. **The Sou'Wester Restaurant and Gift Shop**, Peggy's Cove
20. **Trattoria Della Nonna Ristaurante e Pizzaria**, Lunenburg
21. **Trellis Café**, Hubbards
22. **Trout Point Lodge of Nova Scotia**, East Kemptville
23. **White Point Beach Resort**, White Point
24. **Woodpile Carvings and Café**, Liverpool

RESTAURANT GUIDE

Except for Trout Point Lodge, which is just off the beaten path in East Kemptville, all of the eateries featured in this book are located along Nova Scotia's ruggedly scenic Lighthouse Route, where incredible views of the Atlantic Ocean are just around every corner.

The Biscuit Eater Café and Bookseller (#1 on map)
16 Orchard Street, Mahone Bay
(902) 624-2665
Light fare, local and organic when possible, fair trade coffee, and an impressive bakery
(Kafka Cookies, page 64)

Charlotte Lane Café (#2 on map)
13 Charlotte Lane, Shelburne
(902) 875-3314
Fine dining; seafood, meat, and Swiss specialties
(Scallops with Orange Sesame Ginger Drizzle, page 37)

Chez Bruno's Café and Bistro (#3 on map)
222 Main Street, Yarmouth
(902) 742-0031
Understated elegance in both décor and menu; focus on seafood
(Pork Steak with Pommery Mustard Sauce, page 43)

Dauphinee Inn (#4 on map)
167 Shore Club Road, Hubbards
(902) 857-1790
An old-world inn with a beautifully appointed dining room; focus on seafood
(Seafood Primavera, page 20)

Fleur de Sel Restaurant et Maison (#5 on map)
53 Montague Street, Lunenburg
1-877-723-7258
Fine dining in an award-winning dining room; traditional French cuisine with local flavours
(Scallops with Fava Bean Purée, page 34)

Fredie's Fantastic Fish House (#6 on map)
5280 St. Margaret's Bay Road, Upper Tantallon
(902) 826-9666
Take-out fish dishes; outstanding fish and chips with hand-cut french fries
(Lobster Rolls, page 26)

The Kilted Grillhouse (#7 on map)
3017 Highway 332, Bayport
(902) 764-3000
Pig roasts, local beef, and amazing ribs in a fun, casual environment
(Mako Shark Bites, page 2)

Kiwi Café (#8 on map)
19 Pleasant Street, Chester
(902) 275-1492
Internationally influenced comfort food in casual surroundings
(Thai Squash Soup, page 9)

Lane's Privateer Inn (#9 on map)
27 Bristol Avenue, Liverpool
(902) 354-3456
Family inn featuring local food and local flavours; traditional, broad menu
(Nova Scotia Lamb with Cranberry-Blueberry Compote, page 40)

Large Marge's Diner (#10 on map)
200 Lincoln Street, Lunenburg
(902) 634-4521
Retro diner menu with homestyle cooking in comfy casual surroundings
(Homemade Fishcakes, page 4)

Lothar's Café (#11 on map)
149 Water Street, Shelburne
(902) 875-3697
Hearty German cuisine in casual surroundings
(Strawberry Chicken Salad with Citrus Poppy Seed Dressing, page 53)

Magnolia's Grill (#12 on map)
128 Montague Street, Lunenburg
(902) 634-3287
Made-from-scratch comfort food with surprising international twists and an ever-changing list of soups and daily specials
(Shrimp and Smoked Salmon Pasta, page 23)

Oak Island Resort (#13 on map)
36 Treasure Drive, Western Shore
1-800-565-5075
Full-service resort and convention center with
elegant fine dining
(Planked Maple Salmon with Port-Balsamic Glaze,
page 30)

Oliver Southwoods (#14 on map)
7532 St. Margaret's Bay Road, Boutiliers Point
1-866-766-2233
Fine dining; classic cooking with everything from scratch
(Baked Alaska with Burnt Sugar Rum Sauce, page 57)

The Quarterdeck Beachside Villas and Grill (#15 on map)
Summerville Beach, Port Mouton
1-800-565-1199
Excellent seafood at an out-of-the-way resort
(Shrimp and Scallop Stuffed Lobster Tails, page 29)

The Rope Loft (#16 on map)
Front Harbour, Chester
(902) 275-3430
Casual, relaxed atmosphere; choice of pub, dining room,
or patio deck right on the dock
(Mediterranean Shrimp, page 16)

Salt Shaker Deli (#17 on map)
124 Montague Street, Lunenburg
(902) 640-3434
Upscale, progressive deli fare with international flair
(Smoked Haddock and Seafood Chowder, page 10)

Seaside Shanty Restaurant & Chowder House
(#18 on map)
5315 Highway 3, Chester Basin
(902) 275-2246
Quaint, casual seaside dining; famous for incredible
chowders
(Nova Scotia Blueberry Grunt, page 60)

The Sou'Wester Restaurant and Gift Shop (#19 on map)
178 Peggy's Point Road, Peggy's Cove
(902) 823-2561
Located right beside the famous Peggy's Cove lighthouse;
focus on seafood
(Baby Back Ribs with Hickory Smoke Barbecue Sauce,
page 46)

Trattoria Della Nonna Ristaurante e Pizzaria (#20 on map)
9 King Street, Lunenburg
(902) 640-3112
Classic Italian cuisine with local ingredients and fine wine
(Classic Italian Osso Bucco, page 49)

Trellis Café (#21 on map)
22 Main Street, Hubbards
(902) 857-1188
A real community kitchen feel—home-cooked meals with
local ingredients, on-site bakery, live entertainment
(South Shore Bumbleberry Crisp, page 62)

Trout Point Lodge of Nova Scotia (#22 on map)
189 Trout Point Road, East Kemptville
(902) 761-2142
World-class cooking school and resort with international
acclaim; cuisine combines modern and classic styles
using local produce
(Ruisseau Oysters in Fresh Tomato Marinade, page 15)

White Point Beach Resort (#23 on map)
75 White Point Road, White Point
1-800-565-5068
Seaside resort with a great seafood menu
(Maple Curry Chicken Ravioli, page 50)

Woodpile Carvings and Café (#24 on map)
181 Main Street, Liverpool
(902) 354-4495
Free-trade organic coffee, daily lunch specials, and
fabulous woodcarvings from local artist Elizabeth Brown
(Cinnamon Rolls, page 67)

SOUTH SHORE FOOD RESOURCE DIRECTORY

These are suppliers that are used and recommended by our contributors and/or the author.

ARTISAN BAKERIES

Boulangerie La Vendéenne
7651 Highway 3, RR 2
Mahone Bay
(902) 624-0560
www.boulangerielavendeenne.com

Julien's Pâtisserie, Bakery & Café
43 Queen Street
Chester
(902) 275-2324
www.juliens.ca

La Have Bakery
3391 Highway 331
LaHave
(902) 688-2908 (LaHave location)
(902) 624-1420 (Mahone Bay location)

FARMERS' MARKETS

Hubbards Farmers' Market
Hubbards Barn and Community Park
57 Highway 3
Hubbards
Open Saturdays 8 AM to 12 PM,
May to October
www.hubbardsfarmersmarket.com

Lunenburg Farmers' Market
Lunenburg Community Centre
Victoria Road and Green Street
Lunenburg
Open Thursdays 8 AM to 12 PM,
May to October
www.lunenburgfarmersmarket.com

MAPLE SYRUP

Maplewood Maple Syrup & Christmas Trees
RR 1
Barss Corner
(902) 644-3358

POULTRY

Thousand Hills Farm
375 South Ohio Road
Yarmouth
(902) 749-0835
www.thousandhillsfarm.ca

SEAFOOD

Eel Lake Oyster Farm
P.O. Box 185
Ste. Anne du Ruisseau
(902) 648-3472
www.ruisseauoysters.com

Indian Point Marine Farms
RR 2
Mahone Bay
(902) 624-6472
www.indianpointmussels.ca

Shatford's By The Sea
731 Highway 329
Fox Point
(902) 857-9562
www.shatfordlobster.com

WINERIES

Lunenburg County Winery
813 Walburne Road
Newburne
(902) 644-2415
www.canada-wine.com

Petite Riviere Vineyards
1300 Italy Cross Road
Crousetown
(902) 693-3033
www.petiterivierewines.ca